Christianity

Under

Persecution

Author's Notes

When looking at the history of Christianity in the world with all its ups and downs, one can easily detect that persecution, particularly in Iran, has always been constant in the lives of its believers. Cultural, political, and social structures have forced them through various challenges. Over the past 20 centuries, believers in Iran have had little to no freedom to express their opinions as well as their faith. In addition, believers in Iran, often through assault from other people groups within the country, have encountered persecution to the point of harassment and torture now more than ever.

Through globalization, cultural exchange, and ideas that came with them over the past few decades, it was expected that the amount of pressure and harassment facing Christians would decrease. Studies show, however, that the torture and murder of Christians has only increased over this time period.

Because persecution is such a significant topic for Farsi speaking Christians, specifically those that are directly affected by it, I have decided to take a brief look at persecution and its various perspectives, whether it be from God's Word or from personal experience, and confront the different aspects of persecution with you all. Here it is necessary to take a moment to thank those loved ones in my life, who have always been my source of encouragement and partnered with me throughout this journey of writing.

My dear Karineh, who has always been my intellectual and spiritual support and who was responsible for making the finals reviews of this work; Gohar, who faithfully compiled my writings; Shabnam, for creating the layout and cover design; and Mahyar for performing all the editing. I thank and appreciate all of these dear friends and thank the Lord for using them for His ministry.

Pastor Firouz
November 2017

CONTENTS

Introduction to Analyzing Persecution

What is persecution? Persecution means hostility and ill-treatment, especially because of one's race, political stance, or religious beliefs; to oppress or harass.

Using this definition, can anyone who falls into trouble and hardships use this word for their particular situation? The answer is both yes and no. Simply put, whoever is facing the reality of serious oppression is under persecution. But the main point which we will discuss is persecution as a result of righteousness according to the Bible.

Perhaps due to the wrong decisions that you have made in your lives, you have fallen into particular hardships and are presently facing the consequences of those decisions. Perhaps in the home, society, the workplace, or even perhaps in facing different issues, rules, or politics of the government you have found yourself in hardship. Perhaps you have fallen into fleshly hardships, mental instability, depression, or economic failures. There is no question that these are all considered hardships; however, they are not the main topic of our discussion, or better to say, these hardships do not make up genuine persecution (which the Bible points to). Our discussion will focus on the Bible's definition of persecution, which results from performing just acts.

Explaining the Biblical Concept of Persecution

It is worth mentioning that I, according to the teachings of the Bible, consider no particular problem to be inferior, and I know that some of these problems coming from out of our decision making scope. Problems either come from our personal decisions, someone else's decisions, or surrounding influences. Our focus, however, is on the meaning of persecution as found in the Bible.

According to the Bible, persecution refers to the problems and hardships that come in the form of cruelty inflicted regardless of one's opinion, color, race, or place of living. Persecution refers to the hardships that come as a result of standing for the truth, standing for what is right, for faithfulness to God's Word, and for faith in Jesus Christ.

We see this truth within the first few pages of the Bible, which we consider to be the first few pages of human history. In Genesis 4:4, we see that Abel obeys God's Word. His obedience irritated his brother Cain who did not obey God's Word and this hatred resulted in the murder of Abel the one who stood for what is right. Here more questions arise: what exactly is right? What is truth? Often we hear of terms such as "goodness" and "righteousness," but what exactly do these terms mean?

Romans 3:10 emphasizes that not a single person is good or righteous and that only God has these qualities (Deuteronomy 32:4). Therefore, another question arises that if only God is good, then why do we undergo persecution for goodness and righteousness? It is in the answer to this question that the glory, majesty, depth, and greatness of God's love is shown to us, particularly in the first verses of the Gospel of John. Philippians 2 also sheds light on this matter for us. Because Jesus Christ paid the price for my sin, His righteousness and goodness have been bestowed upon me. Therefore, in the eyes of God, I am seen as holy, righteous, pure. God cannot see us this way without the blood of Jesus Christ, which is what cleanses us of our sins (1 Corinthians 15:3, Romans 3:22-27). Therefore, in Christ and because of Christ I can put on His righteousness and goodness and live in His likeness.

The matter of persecution begins with Galatians 2:20-21 which says, "I am crucified with Christ: nevertheless I live; yet not I, but Christ liveth in me: and the life which I now live in the flesh I live by the faith of the Son of God, who loved me, and gave himself for me. I do not frustrate the grace of God: for if righteousness come by the law, then Christ is dead in vain." Therefore, because the world hated Christ and righteousness, it will also hate whoever is like Christ.

Jesus makes this point in John 15:18-19 which says, "If the world hate you, ye know that it hated me before it hated you. If ye were of the world, the world would love his own: but because ye are not of the world, but I have chosen you out of the world, therefore the world hateth you."

Jesus explained that the world hated Him because He proclaimed the truth; therefore, the world will hate those who are his disciples and will treat them the same way that they treated Jesus. It is because of this connection to Jesus that, according to the UN census, 110,000 Christians from all over the world are murdered every year. These Christians were murdered for being like Jesus. Here it is necessary for me to point out an important truth for some of the readers.

Some people believe that becoming a Christian means having all your desires fulfilled and receiving the freedom to do whatever you wish. This will never happen! If you consider yourself to be a Christian, and you have never faced persecution because of your faith, something is wrong. Jesus said that, "In the world ye shall have tribulation" (John 16:33). In Matthew 10:16 Jesus clearly states: "Behold, I send you forth as sheep in the midst of wolves..." and we all know that the result is horrifying.

The second area in which we as Christians face persecution is in our faithfulness to God and His Word. In some religions, their stance on persecution, deceit, white lies, and even changing your faith in order to save your life is acceptable, but God's Word says that only the truth should proceed out of your mouth. Matthew 5:37 clearly says, "But let your communication be, Yea, yea; Nay, nay: for whatsoever is more than these cometh of evil."

Allow me to elaborate. This subject of faithfulness to God's Word is directly correlated to the trials we face in our Christian life. 1 Peter 4:12 says, "Beloved, think it not strange concerning the fiery trial which is to try you, as though some strange thing happened unto you." This verse is telling us that our faith, love, and faithfulness to the Lord is shown in times of testing. Therefore, persecution as depicted in the Bible tells us that we as followers of Christ partake in His afflictions and hardships and allow ourselves to suffer the way He did, because we are indeed Christians.

A History of the Persecution of the Church

Let us take a look at the history of the persecution of the church. The book of Acts gives us a history from the beginning of the church, as well as the beginning of its persecution. Each of the instances recorded in the book of Acts serves as an excellent example of the work of the Holy Spirit and shows us how to react in similar instances.

Before we continue, it must be said that persecution is a blessing to the church. Please do not be quick to judge this statement. It is not my intention to make general or cliché statements, I only wish to convey the meaning of blessing in the midst of persecution as shown in God's Word through the book of Acts. The persecution of Jesus Christ (when people called Him possessed and a friend of sinners) was the very first manifestation of the persecution of the church. Note that being persecuted for your faith can come in many forms, such as being fired from your job, harassed by your family members, insulted, wrongly accused, or even killed. Jesus Christ performed great miracles before the eyes of thousands of Jews. In the span of three and a half years, He completely extinguished disease within a single area, He healed the blind and those with leprosy, raised the dead to life and cast out demons. However, He was simply accused of accomplishing these miracles through the power of Satan. Making these kinds of accusations against someone who had society's best interest in mind is in itself a severe form of persecution.

Jesus faced many forms of persecution throughout His life, and even died while being persecuted on the cross. Nevertheless, this was all a part of God's plan so that Jesus could pay the price for our sins. In the end, Christ's death and resurrection shattered the expectations of the disciples and, with this daring act, Christ allowed hem to see God's amazing power.

The disciples were those who, in the events prior to Jesus' death, would flee in the face of danger and would even go as far as to deny Him. Peter was one of these disciples. In Acts 2:14, however, Peter undergoes a significant change. He gained the courage to stand before an astonished crowd of people and preach to them with the power of the Holy Spirit (Acts 2:22-29). After seeing the resurrected Christ, Peter changed and began to proclaim truth and righteousness like Jesus.

The bold words spoken as a result of having faith in our Savior Jesus Christ will lead to miracles taking place in our lives, and will in turn fuel the fire of our faith. Where faith grows, however, so does persecution. As we see in Peter's first sermon, 3,000 people repented and put their faith in Jesus Christ (Acts 2:14-41).

Later on, we see that 5,000 men (if we include women and children, an estimated 20,000 people) put their faith in Jesus Christ (Acts 4:4). In both his sermons Peter proclaimed that the people, in their ignorance, killed Jesus Christ and needed to repent immediately so that they may be saved. Meanwhile, miracles (such as speaking in tongues and healing the lame) took place and began to fuel the fire of persecution (which had already begun to take form).

The Jewish leaders and their soldiers then came and arrested the disciples. Why? Because seeing people proclaim the truth and doing what was right brought fear upon the Jewish leaders

(Acts 4). The day after the disciples were arrested, they were asked: "By what power, or by what name, have ye done this? Then Peter, filled with the Holy Ghost, said unto them, Ye rulers of the people, and elders of Israel...If we this day be examined of the good deed done to the impotent man, by what means he is made whole; Be it known unto you all, and to all the people of Israel, that by the name of Jesus Christ of Nazareth, whom ye crucified, whom God raised from the dead, even by him doth this man stand here before you whole" (Acts 4:7-10). Because they had no other choice, the Jewish leaders were forced to release them.

It was, however, only the beginning. During the first three centuries, Christianity faced ten horrific kinds of persecution. When Peter and John were summoned again, the threats that they received had come to an end and they were finally released.

It was not long, however, until the threats increased and eventually led to the martyrdom of James and Stephen. After several devoted followers of Christ were arrested, authorities went from city to city and house to house arresting others like them.

Today's Christians are persecuted for the same reasons that those of the first century were. These Christians, including those in Iran, hear the Gospel and as a result follow the path of truth and righteousness, which contradicts the political agenda of religious leaders.

The harassment of Christians continued until 67, during the reign of the sixth emperor of the Rome Nero who essentially made himself into a god. Therefore, this subject of persecution has gradually turned into a matter of politics and government activity. Because Christians believed that their God differed from the "Roman god" (or the emperor), it caused them to undermine the emperor's authority. As a result, they faced terrible persecution and, like candles in the darkness, burned so that their light would shine. Over time persecution took many different forms. Christians were thrown into dens of wild animals, sawed in half, wrapped in animal skins to experience a slow and gradual death, have their belongings pillaged, as well as other means of persecution. The Roman emperor Domitian commanded Christians to be boiled to death in oil, burned, or covered in molten liquid. These methods were carried on by succeeding Roman emperors. These examples of persecution show how Satan, through his subjects, can have an effect on the church. Even today in the twenty-first century we see this effect, particularly in Muslim countries. Persecutors have proudly posted videos on social media of Christians being burned alive and thrown into pits.

God does not enjoy such horrific persecution taking place. He commanded Adam and Eve not to eat of the tree of the knowledge of good and evil. The day that they ate of the fruit, sin, as well as the consequences of disobeying God came upon humanity. Many ask why God put that tree in the garden to begin with. If that tree had not existed, there would be no temptation and, therefore, no sin. We must remember, however, that God never deprives humans of their free will and ability to choose. If the tree (or anything similar to it) never existed, then the ability to choose and, in turn, the entire concept of freedom would not exist.

Humans need to understand who God is and what it means to have Him reign in our hearts. The one true God who has revealed Himself through His Word greatly respects our right to choose. Therefore, sin, the curse upon creation, and the consequences thereof (including the hatred of light and righteousness) all came as a result of human choice.

The first example of these consequences that was recorded in human history is found in the story of the sacrifices made by Cain and Abel. Although God had told them exactly what He wanted them to sacrifice, Cain still chose to undermine God's command. The hatred and spite which then filled Cain caused him to murder his own brother.

Persecution in the Home and in Society

I clearly remember the time that I became a believer. Although I was being mistreated by the government, my persecution came mainly from my family. My uncle would assault me in the middle of the night, and I was faced with no other choice but to leave my home. Even my mother would take my plate of food and wash the plate off several times, saying that I had become polluted and that I had become "Armenian" (they were unaware that Armenians were not a religious group but a nation, and that it is impossible for a person to change their nationality). Let us not forget that the persecution of the church body has always existed and will continue to exist. Sometimes persecution comes from the government, sometimes from religious groups, and quite often from within your own home.

Persecution in the home usually begins with threats and later on leads to rising tension and pressure from family members. Among the examples that I have personally witnessed, one father became legally deprived of seeing his three children after his wife complained to the authorities about his decision to become a Christian.

Remember that persecution does not always mean being boiled in hot oil or killed. Other methods of persecuting the church involve the spreading of false doctrine, which is more terrible than all previously mentioned forms of persecution. A church teaching false doctrine is often described as "a church without Jesus." A portion of Revelation 3:1-4 states, "...I know thy works, that thou hast a name that thou livest, and art dead..."

You are probably wondering what is meant by this statement. In order to properly understand this statement, we must step away from history. In the third century, the Roman emperor Constantine, in pursuit of the dreams that he had, ruled the empire in such a way that the "religion" of Christianity became the official religion of the empire.

Pay close attention to the phrase: "the religion of Christianity." You can guess that in such a disturbed market, how many false teachers unworthy imposters came "in the name of Jesus" and instead spoiled the church and took advantage of it. From this behavior sprung a time of frightening darkness for the church, the result of which was the Inquisition, the Crusades, as well as the right to sell the land of heaven.

Many religious imposters introduced Christ as someone who was always occupied; therefore, saints were chosen so that people could go pray to them instead. Unfortunately, if a lie is repeated enough, people will eventually start to believe it, and thus under these circumstances, the church, the Bible, and Christianity altogether began to take on a much different form—one without Jesus Christ. In some of these churches, the meaning of persecution has changed completely, even to the extent that some Catholic priests understand persecution to be purposefully tying barbed wire or blades to their bodies under their long, rough robes to inflict pain on themselves. Today some Christians mistakenly believe that persecution comes from spouses, parents, in-laws, or other family members. This is not true! The cause of persecution is living a pure and holy life in the midst of a dark and unforgiving world like Jesus did (1 Peter 2:21, 2 Timothy 3:12).

The church was created to make people aware of the terrifying future that lies ahead without Jesus Christ, and to proclaim the good news of the Gospel that all may hear of how there is no other name in heaven or on earth by which we may receive the forgiveness of sins. Therefore, if people accept the Gospel, they will receive salvation and eternal life in the presence of the Lord.

The main reason why people hesitate to repent and believe in Jesus Christ is that they fear persecution. It is truly impossible for someone to read the Word of God and not recognize the authority of Jesus Christ and bow before Him. God's Word speaks clearly about Jesus Christ and salvation. It has not left anything unexplained nor has it made any room for excuses. Although people are faced with the truth, because of their fear of persecution, they refuse to accept Jesus Christ as their Savior. This persecution can come in the form of being rejected by family members, losing a job, being cut out of an inheritance, coming into conflict with the government, and other such forms.

Jesus Christ is the only one in the world who practiced what He preached. Jesus says in John 15:13, "Greater love hath no man than this, that a man lay down his life for his friends." In the following verse He says, "You are my friends..." In the end, Jesus practiced what He preached and gave His life on the cross for our sins. Jesus went through all the forms of persecution that were previously stated; He was rejected by His own people, disciples, and even His own family. For this reason Jesus says in Matthew 10:34 "...I came not to send peace, but a sword." This verse refers to the clashing of darkness and light, what is wrong and what is right, deceit and truth. Jesus did not tell us to draw our swords, instead He says that others will draw their swords against us. We must, however, bless them. The truth is that if believers do not commit to and obey God's Word, and in their faith and actions are not faithful witnesses of Jesus Christ, they will not see persecution.

Persecution in the Free World

Many people think that because they are the citizens of a Muslim, Buddhist, or other religious country, they are restricted from the benefits of the "free world." They think that they cannot read the Bible, pray in restaurants, or share the Gospel with their new coworkers openly and freely. These people, however, are greatly misinformed. Persecution for true churches has no end. As a matter of fact, not only are these "free countries" not actually free, but also they, much like the non-Christian countries, openly proclaim their animosity for Christ, because the entire world is controlled by Satan. He is the father of lies and hates goodness and righteousness and persuades his followers to hate the truth and righteousness. America claims to be one of the most free countries in the world; however, when it comes to the Gospel of Jesus Christ, they quickly change their stance in an unbelievable way. For example, promoting the Bible in school is illegal. Also, if a Christian student decides to bow their head and pray in the name of Jesus at lunchtime, they may be discouraged from doing so. If a Muslim student, however, at the same place decides to lay out their prayer mat there is no problem. If a teacher dares to talk about Jesus Christ during class, the teacher will definitely get fired.

A friend of mine who is an emergency room physician recounted one of his hospital experiences for me. A patient was brought into the emergency room for treatment. While he was being care for, he opened up to the physician about his tragic life. This man gave all of his worldly effort in order to have a good life. In the end, however, he felt defeated and disappointed by the future. He then attempted suicide and was hospitalized as a result. It was clear that there was an emptiness in his heart that can only be filled by Jesus Christ. My friend told me that he really wanted to talk to him about Jesus Christ; however, it was plain as day that he would definitely get fired because of it. He was absolutely right. In the workplace, whether it be run by the government or not, no one has permission to speak about Jesus Christ. Notice that all of the emphasis is on Jesus Christ. At the same time, if you are associated with any specific group, you can speak about it freely, hold a particular event regarding it, and even take invitations to work and give them to all of your coworkers. You can even tell them what group you are associated with and why the event is being held. But If you want to invite someone for church on Sunday, however, you will have to answer to all of your superiors

Therefore, when it comes to talking about standing for that which is right and true—Jesus Christ—there is no difference between America and Iran or Afghanistan. Perhaps there are those who think that families that live in free countries have better relationships among themselves. According to my experience, however, as well as the experiences of those around me, this is definitely not the case. For example, a Christian brother told me that before he became a believer, he was a sociable jokester. He was considered the life of the party. Sometimes he would even tell jokes that were offensive or that would disrespect women to the point of being superfluous. When he encountered Jesus Christ and repented, however, many things changed in his life. One of the things that he gave up was his excessive joking. At the first family gathering after his conversion, he told his friends and family about what Jesus had done for him. He told me that everyone had gathered around him and asked if he were sick, depressed, or if something else were wrong. He responded by telling them that his change in behavior was a result of believing in Jesus Christ. Both friends and family, however, responded by insulting and humiliating him in their own ways.

In the end, heartbroken, he left the gathering. To this day, his relationships are still affected by his decision to believe in Jesus. Nevertheless, he still loves them as he always has. Of course, his heart did not ache for himself but rather for his family and the fact that they do not realize how mistaken they are in mocking the truth and his standing for Jesus Christ. His family is plagued by a mindset that believing in Jesus leads to close-mindedness.

Unfortunately, even some believers are plagued by this mindset that others should not be so closed-minded. These are the believers who say that there is no problem with having one glass of alcohol and that even Jesus turned water into wine. These people, being uninformed, misinterpret the Bible and then teach others. Christ said in Matthew 18:6 "But whosoever shall offend one of these little ones which believe in me, it were better for him that a millstone were hanged about his neck, and that he were drowned in the depth of the sea." The Lord makes it clear that those who offend His children will be judged. To those who say that there is no problem with having one glass of beer, or one shot of whiskey or liquor, I have to say that I know for a fact that Jesus Christ would not command or encourage anything that with a single ounce can kill a million brain cells.

Even in free countries, standing for Jesus among family members is difficult and causes problems. Indeed, this old Persian poem which says **"in order to avoid shaming yourself, conform to this world"** has become a template for the lives of many people in the world today. God's Word, however, tells us in 1 Peter 2:11; "Dearly beloved, I beseech you as strangers and pilgrims, abstain from fleshly lusts, which war against the soul." Simply put, the Lord tells us to refrain from becoming like the world and to be separate.

I want to point to a particular example of this topic of being separate that I have seen repeatedly in my years of ministering in a free country. Even in free countries, like America, when there are hardships because of having faith in Jesus Christ, it is typically because the believer focuses on his family's approval instead of God's approval. I know a lady who a few years ago was searching for a Farsi-speaking pastor and happened to come across my name. During her encounter with me, this dear lady explained the events that had taken place in her life: "A few months ago I had very severe cancer and went into a coma. In a dream I saw a man in a long robe with a very lovely, luminous face standing in the corner of the room that I was sleeping in. In between sleeping and waking He said to me: 'Arise, I have healed you.' In that instant I opened my eyes and saw that my family members were all looking at me— happy to see that I had awoken." She continued: "At that moment one of my family members who was beside me said: 'Grandma, how interesting, just a few minutes ago two people from church were here and they were praying for you.' After a few days I was released from the hospital in perfect health and the doctors had no explanation for my recovery. After a while, my life returned to its normal routine until two weeks before I contacted you." She said: "Two weeks ago I was in my living room sitting on the couch waiting for my grandchildren to come home from school. There was a knock at the door, and I got up to answer it. To my surprise, at the door was the same man that I saw in my dream at the hospital who healed me! I knew exactly who He was—Jesus Christ. He was standing at the door as luminous as the last time I saw him." (This lady repeated the matter over and over again until she was sure that I completely understood what she had said). She then added: "His presence was as real as your presence sitting right here in front of me." I asked this lady: "Well, eventually what did Christ say to you? He must have had something important to say if He came to you personally. This shows how valuable you are to Christ."

At first she thought that I was simply being polite by asking further, but when she saw that I genuinely wanted to know more, she continued: "Christ didn't say anything at all, He only put a pocket watch in my hand and smiled. He then got up and left the house. Upon his leaving, both the light that filled my house and the watch that was placed in my hand faded away." She continued: "I invited you to come here and tell me what the encounter means." Without delay I told her that the Lord's message for her is that time is short, and it is time for you to repent and believe in Jesus Christ." The first thing that this dear lady said in response was: "What will happen to my reputation with my children and grandchildren? They'll ask how could grandma decide to become a Christian at this age?" In the midst of all of these beautiful events that the Lord brought into this woman's life, most important of all the complete healing of her cancer, she was worriedabout what her family would say! This all took place in the free country of America, which shows that even those who have complete access to the truth may find an excuse to reject Christ.

Hardships as a result of our own decisions

We should not forget that the results of our decisions are like a double-edged sword that not only affect our lives but also the lives of others. For example, if someone decides to drink alcohol and drive while he is drunk, the result of that decision will be that he has to face the law. It is a two-edged sword. One edge is that he must face the law, the other edge is the harm that he causes himself.

There are many examples in the Bible of different hardships that come from personal decisions;

for example, God gave Abraham a promise that Sarah would have a child. After a long period of time without conceiving a child, Sarah decided to help fulfill God's promise. Therefore, Abraham took Sarah's handmaid Hagar, conceived a child with her, and named that child Ishmael. The descendants of Ishmael and the descendants of Isaac have been at war for centuries and continue till this day--the war between the Arab nations and Israel.

The results of disobeying God's commands have always been horrific. To this day people still reject the gift of salvation through Jesus Christ because of their fear of persecution. Throughout the Bible and the history of the nation of Israel, the truths that I have mentioned above have repeated, and we see that hardships ultimately come as a result of the decisions that we as humans have made.

Persecution as a result of spiritual warfare

The story of the life of Job is the best example of persecution in the Bible. The persecution that was brought upon him did not come as a result of his sin or financial status. The only reason that he was persecuted was so that you and I could be aware of what is happening behind the scenes. Job was a God-fearing man who served the Lord with complete faithfulness. His life was based on God's Word even to the point of continually making burnt sacrifices for the unintentional sins of his children.

All of a sudden, he underwent hardships and persecution that stupefied him and his peers. Why did Job undergo persecution? Because the battle is over standing for truth and righteousness. It is between darkness and light—a battle that has always been and will continue until the end of time. The issue was that Satan accused Job of not following God for the sake of truth and righteousness; instead, Satan claimed that Job followed God for financial and worldly benefits. Satan was sure that, if God took away the blessings and the protection that He had given Job, he would deny God. There are four main principles in the book of Job. First, there was much going on behind the scenes that Job did not know about. Second, there is a spiritual battle that Job is involved in a battle in which he could not declare neutrality. Third, by seeing how Job's friends react to his hardships, we can learn much about how others respond to our persecution. Fourth, we must pay attention to how God responds to our persecution.

In a single day, Job underwent many afflictions, including the death of his children. While encountering these afflictions, Job said: "...the Lord gave, and the Lord hath taken away; blessed be the name of the Lord" (Job 1:21). These are not empty words coming out of the mouth of an oblivious, purposeless man. Job was a wise man that people came to for direction. The words that he spoke were not based on blind ignorance, but rather on faith in God, His decisions, and His working in Job's life. Job knew that God's ways are right, and for this reason Job said: "For I know that my redeemer liveth, and that he shall stand at the latter day upon the earth" (Job 19:25). Job did not say these words in vain, but rather in accordance with Romans 8:28 which was written centuries later through the Holy Spirit. Job had faith that "...all things work together for good to them that love God, to them who are the called according to his purpose."

This verse brings us to the question: "Can we say that persecution is a type of blessing?" In response we must say that: unrighteousness and injustice towards believers in Jesus Christ in it- self is not a blessing;

however, the Lord works all things together for our good according to His promise in Romans 8:28. Therefore, it can be said that persecution bring blessings upon the church, the most important of these blessings is the growth of the church. Humans do not know that God has good intentions, and because they disobey God's commands, they fall prey to spiritual blindness. They then seek their own selfish desires.

Approaching Persecution in the Psalms

Before getting to the blessings of the church that come from persecution, I want us to take a look at the book of Psalms. The individual psalms were written by a few different people. The chapters of interest are those that were written by David. The book of Psalms is not a history book, nor does it explain the law, nor does it give recommendations for your social relationships. The reason why this book is so popular among most people is that the writers, with the direction of the Holy Spirit and without putting up any facade, express their emotions, whether they be beautiful or ugly.

These people had feelings of fear, panic, sadness, affliction, happiness, anger, vengeance, and other such emotions that every human faces in their lives. Psalms 22 and 31 are examples of the questions that humans have for God, and Psalms 34 and 35 describe the world's hatred for justice as well as their desire for persecution of the righteous. Psalms 41 and 42 are examples of Christ's perfection, righteousness, and persecution. Finally, Psalms 58 and 69 are about the persecution of King David.

When a believer faces persecution because of standing for truth and righteousness, all of the human emotions previously mentioned are logical and understandable. It is here that we are unable to hide our emotions from God, for He sees our hearts and knows all. It is better to share these emotions with God without putting up a facade.

Hardships as a result of humans being separated from God

Another reason for hardships, in our discussion is the human's disconnection with God—the source of blessings. Without God's protection, a pathway for Satan to harm us opens. The Bible compares sin to scissors that cuts the thread of our relationship with the Lord. Simply stated, because we have rebelled against God's blessings, we now live in a cursed world. Many people ask why bad things happen to good people. These questions have the wrong basis because good people do not exist.

The probability of falling into sin is true for all humans. Life in sin leads to spiritual death, and given the nature of sin, no one can say that he has sinned less than others. It is like a person saying that he has died less than others, or like someone who has drowned in an ocean comparing himself to someone who has drowned in a swimming pool. We should never expect anything good to come from the existence of humans. All goodness comes from the spirit of God. It is for this reason that the Bible emphasizes that Jesus Christ is the only answer for the issue of humans being separated from God.

Blessing: The Product of Persecution

First Peter 4:12-14 says that it is because of the name of Jesus that we undergo persecution. It does not say that we undergo persecution because of anything else. It is only because of the one who claims that He is truth and righteousness, Jesus Christ, and by bearing His name that we undergo persecution. Why does the Word of God place so much emphasis on these principles? It is because Jesus said that He came so that we may know truth and be set free (John 8:32). Even Pilate asked what truth is (John 18:38). Jesus Christ gives the answer to this question time and time again—that He is "the way, the truth, and the life" (John 14:6). He also tells us that if we do not put our faith in Him, we will die in our sins. Pay attention to how verse 14 takes form between the other verses. If we see ersecution because of Christ or because of the truth (which are one in the same), then according to verse 12 we should not be surprised as if something strange happened to us. We should expect this persecution to come. This persecution comes first, to test you; second, so that you can partake in the persecution and hardships of Christ; and third, so that the first two can result in blessings. How does this process happen?

The first blessing: If Peter and John never underwent persecution, perhaps they never would have had the chance to witness to the great leaders of the Jewish council.

The second blessing: Peter and John waited patiently for God to work. God did work and they gained the victory.

The third blessing: By trusting in God's ways, they took steps towards knowing Him.

The fourth blessing: Because they trusted, they saw God work and knew Him better. They then became courageous; and, instead of sitting back, stood in the face of persecution.

Today's church, upon encountering persecution, instantly becomes frightened and decides to sit back and in protest say that others are notamong the persecuted churches until they see how barbarically believers are treated. Is there, however, anything more barbaric than what was done to Jesus? Peter dared to proclaim that in the name of Jesus Christ whom the Jews killed did they perform their miracles.

That same Jesus still takes the sins of people upon himself today. Among our own people, many men and women who are zealous for the Lord and who love Him have mistakenly fallen down the path of destruction. These zealous people think that if they act against Christ they are honoring God, and, if they eliminate Christians, they have fulfilled their obligation. We must, with the love of God, help these people. The only things that are necessary to help these people are knowing Jesus Christ properly and having courage. These people must be told that they are completely wrong. Kicking at the nails of the cross will result in nothing but damage to one's self. It takes a lot of courage to proclaim this to these people. They must be ready to risk their lives and not be afraid of anything. It is for this reason that in 1 Peter 4:14 the apostle Peter tells us that if we see persecution because of Jesus Christ and that which is the truth, happiness, blessing, and honor will be with us.

Paul tells us in 2 Corinthians 12:7-10: "And lest I should be exalted above measure through the abundance of the revelations, there was given to me a thorn in the flesh, the messenger of Satan to buffet me, lest I should be exalted above measure. For this thing I besought the Lord thrice, that it might depart from me. And he said unto me, My grace is sufficient for thee: for my strength is made perfect in weakness. Most gladly therefore will I rather glory in my infirmities, that the power of Christ may rest upon me. Therefore I take pleasure in infirmities, in reproaches, in necessities, in persecutions, in distresses for Christ's sake: for when I am weak, then am I strong."

Paul saw persecution as the agent of both mercy and blessing. Philippians 2:17 tell us: "Yea, and if I be offered upon the sacrifice and service of your faith, I joy, and rejoice with you all."

Paul saw persecution as mercy, something that had been constant all the days of his life. Take a look at 2 Corinthians 6:3-10 where the apostle Paul says, "Giving no offence in any thing, that the ministry be not blamed: But in all things approving ourselves as the ministers of God, in much patience, in afflictions, in necessities, in distresses, In stripes, in imprisonments, in tumults, in labours, in watchings, in fastings;

By pureness, by knowledge, by longsuffering, by kindness, by the Holy Ghost, by love unfeigned, By the word of truth, by the power of God, by the armour of righteousness on the right hand and on the left, By honour and dishonour, by evil report and good report: as deceivers, and yet true; As unknown, and yet well known; as dying, and, behold, we live; as chastened, and not killed; As sorrowful, yet alway rejoicing; as poor, yet making many rich; as having nothing, and yet possessing all things."

Rejoicing in Persecution

Let us take a more accurate look at the meanings of the words "joy" and "happiness." These two words have completely different roots and meanings. "Happiness" for us and those around us can come and go based on things that happen in our lives. For instance, when you find a job you become happy, but when you find out that the salary is low the happiness goes away. When you buy new clothes you become happy, but when you try them on at home and find something wrong with them, your happiness is eliminated. When you first meet your boyfriend or girlfriend, you become happy because on the outside their standards are to your liking. A little further into the relationship, however, when you begin to open up conversation and he or she welcomes you with a smile, your happiness is eliminated when you realize that they have no teeth.

Now let us look at the meaning of the word "joy." Joy is a fruit of the spirit of God that does not change under any circumstance—not even under persecution. Second Corinthians 7:4 states, "Great is my boldness of speech toward you, great is my glorying of you: I am filled with comfort, I am exceeding joyful in all our tribulation." Why? Because my joy for the truth and for that glorious hope of the future is unchangeable. Seeing persecution for truth and righteousness is the reality of the life of one who is a disciple of Jesus Christ. If you pay close attention while reading Colossians 1:23-29, you will understand our glorious hope much better. In this passage Paul proclaims that I rejoice in my persecution because first, I trust in Jesus, and second, my affliction and persecution is because of Christ, therefore, a world that hates Him will see me as a target for their wrath. This statement is not an exaggeration, but rather the bitter reality that the world hates whoever loves and follows Jesus Christ because, in actuality, it hates Jesus Christ himself.

Let us survey the brave people of the Old Testament. Those who stood for the Lord by standing for truth and righteousness faced terrible persecution. During the time of the mighty emperor Nebuchadnezzar, a decree was given that all must worship his statue. Daniel's friends restrained themselves from doing this and said in Daniel 3:17-18, *"If it be so, our God whom we serve is able to deliver us from the burning fiery furnace, and he will deliver us out of thine hand, O king. But if not, be it known unto thee, O king, that we will not serve thy gods, nor worship the golden image which thou hast set up."*

In his old age, Daniel faced persecution by being thrown into a lion's den. The full explanation of this account is found in the Bible, and it is clear that this was not simply a threat but rather an actual occurrence. These accounts remind us that first, no matter how heavy, merciless, or horrifying the persecution may be, God is greater and higher than any circumstance. He is easily capable of changing any circumstance in a moment. Second, in the life of a devout believer, nothing happens without the Lord's permission. According to God's Word in Romans 8:16-17, "The Spirit itself beareth witness with our spirit, that we are the children of God: And if children, then heirs;

heirs of God, and joint-heirs with Christ; if so be that we suffer with Him, that we may be also glorified together." Therefore, if we are the heirs of Christ and partake in His glory, then we must also partake in His hardships and persecution. This relationship with Christ is the reason for the joy of a believer in the midst of persecution. Happiness in this world is dependent on whether or not our desires and dreams are fulfilled. Our joy, however, is because we have Jesus Christ who resurrected from the dead and is sitting on the right hand of God in glory and victory. Our joy has no end because the Lord our King Jesus Christ has no end. We not only believe that He stands with us in our persecution, but also that He is capable of willing our situation to change at any moment and that in the end we will receive our reward from Him.

Victory in Persecution

Another beautiful example in the Old Testament comes from a youth named Joseph who, in honoring God, truth, and righteousness, stood against being tempted by Potiphar's wife to sleep together. Joseph says in Genesis 39:8-9, "...Behold, my master wotteth not what is with me in the house, and he hath committed all that he hath to my hand; There is none greater in this house than I; neither hath he kept back anything from me but thee, because thou art his wife: how then can I do this great wickedness, and sin against God?"

Some men take great pride in this wicked act and talk about it all the time. Because he took a stand, however, Joseph spent sixteen years in jail being persecuted. Joseph could have protested and asked: "My Lord, I have been faithful to you and because of you. Do I deserve to spend the best years of my youth in jail?" Despite his situation, he never protested. Much like Job who said: "...the Lord gave, and the Lord hath taken away; blessed be the name of the Lord" (Job 1:21). Joseph also trusted in God's thoughts, ways, and decisions. What was the result of this bravery? It is facing persecution and seeing that in one night, God changed the circumstances. It is going from prison to being the highest ranking person in Egypt under Pharaoh. Therefore, we can say that joy in Jesus Christ is dependent on being a child of God and will not in any way be lost because of circumstances. Nothing can take it away. Whoever is living a pure and holy life and is following the Lord Jesus Christ will face persecution; however, victory certainly belongs to him because Christ, our Lord and King, is always victorious.

Faithfulness in Persecution

An important point that I want to draw your attention to is the circumstances of those people who start off really well, and with faith, affection, passion, and enthusiasm go forward. Slowly but surely, however, they backslide and fuse with the world. These people don't properly finish their good work.

Regarding this matter, in Mark 13:13 Jesus Christ says, "And ye shall be hated of all men for my name's sake: but he that shall endure unto the end, the same shall be saved." Therefore, continuing in faith is extremely difficult. In our lives we are ever facing persecution. According to the words of Christ, however, we must remain faithful until the end. This good news is found in 2 Corinthians 1:5, which says, "For as the sufferings of Christ abound in us, so our consolation also aboundeth by Christ."

How to Stand in the Face of Persecution

What does it mean to take a stand? Does it mean to stand up and be spectators or to run away from persecution and not recognize it? Unfortunately, today as soon as the smallest form of persecution for the church is detected, suddenly everyone runs to the Lord begging Him to free them from the persecution. If we have faith that blessing is the result of persecution, then we must stand and see what God wants to accomplish with the church through our cooperation and our taking a stand in the midst of this persecution. When Peter and John were in the midst of persecution, an opportunity to witness to the Supreme Council members of the Jewish community was at hand. They beat the Apostle Paul and threw him into prison, but it was there that Paul witnessed to the prison ward at Philippi and, as a result, he and his family received salvation. Paul even gave the Good News to the emperor's guard while in prison.

The Lord's church was founded on persecution. The cross of Jesus Christ began the persecution of the church, which continued in the death of Stephen as well as the successive attacks against believers. Since the beginning, persecution has and always will be with the Lord's true church.

Most importantly, the source of persecution for the true church of Christ is the entire world—not just a specific area. The entire world has a problem with the church of truth. False religions promote the idea that in the name of zeal for the Lord, any indecency or idol worship is acceptable in order to reach their goal. In order to reach their wicked goals they also form a hostility towards Christ.

On the other hand, those who consider hemselves to be wise deny the existence of God the Creator, and in the name of freedom promote immorality. Their freedom is destroyed by their own moral corruption and impure desires. People are free to be homosexual; they are free to mock the Creator of all things; and they are free to, with their own limited thinking, question Him. If only the questions they asked were a result of genuine curiosity and a desire to understand the matter at hand; however, the purpose of their asking is to ridicule everything. They ask questions such as: "If God exists, then why is there so much oppression, misery, starvation, and corruption in the world? Why are there so many disabled children?"

It can be said in response that maybe it is because many people are so drowned in their own selfishness that they can fill their own stockroom with wheat and grain and throw it into the ocean in case the price of wheat goes down, however not be satisfied in giving it to the hungry.

It can also be said in response that maybe it is because there are helpless women who during their pregnancy are beaten, oppressed by their husbands, and are under such mental pressure that they give birth to deformed children. There are many statistics on this that are given by medical societies today. When a mother has an increase in her heart rate due to a moment of sudden fear, the heartbeat of the fetus also skyrockets. Many physicians prescribe music for pregnant mothers. Unfortunately, for many mothers, instead of music the only sounds they hear are the sounds of screaming, profanity, and dis-respect coming from their husbands.

Why does so much oppression and misery exist? Because humans willingly took the gifts that the Lord gave and, with honor, offered them to Satan, making him the ruler of this world. When hearing these words, people make each other feel hopeless concerning the wonderful love of God with the notion that God is condemning them, when in reality they are only condemning themselves. God's eyes are too pure to see that which is bad, unfair, or sinful, let alone take part in it. God gave an opportunity to this world to repent and receive salvation through His only begotten Son Jesus Christ; afterwards, judgement and punishment are certain.

Furthermore, it is necessary to take a stand in the face of persecution with acceptance and patience until God's amazing work is made clear. It is more important to be filled with the Holy Spirit in times of persecution than during any other time, until the thoughts and plans of the Lord are made clear to us through His Spirit. We can then, with complete confidence in the Lord, accept persecution. Jesus Christ said to His disciples in Matthew 10:18-20, "And ye shall be brought before governors and kings for my sake, for a testimony against them and the Gentiles. But when they deliver you up, take no thought how or what ye shall speak: for it shall be given you in that same hour what ye shall speak. For it is not ye that speak, but the Spirit of your Father which speaketh in you." It is necessary to stand bravely in the face of persecution.

Therefore, if we have God's Spirit, we must know that it is not the spirit of fear, but rather as the Bible says in Acts 4:13; "Now when they saw the boldness of Peter and John..." boldness here means to stand in the face of persecution, and to speak the truth—not with consideration, worldly regard, or fear, but rather with love, respect and authority—the same authority that the disciples received from the Lord Jesus Christ. In the face of persecution one must, in complete obedience to the Lord, take a stand. This means to live a life according to God's Word and to stay on His path. A five-year-old child can walk, but he can't find his path. According to God's Word spoken through David in Psalm 119:105 "Thy word is a lamp unto my feet, and a light unto my path." We must live our lives based on the Word of God. It is because true dedication, even in the midst of persecution, means that because one lives according to God's Word, and follows the way of

Christ like the disciples did, the world will hate him. Persecution, hardships and difficulties show the measure of one's faithfulness.

Why Do Churches or the Devout See Persecution?

The church faces persecution because it was chosen to give the saving news of the Gospel to mankind, and to proclaim the Good News to everyone. The devout face persecution because they are the channel through which people receive heavenly blessings. You and I have received healing through the afflictions of Christ, just as we received the Gospel through the persecution of the Apostles (especially Paul, who was the apostle of the nations). We also undergo persecution to bless others. Because of the immense level of persecution that the apostle Paul faced, the years he spent chained in various prisons and tortured in dungeons, we now receive this treasure called the Gospel, by which we learn how to live a pure and holy life.

This process will continue until the rapture of the church. Of course, after the rapture, there will be more terrible forms of persecution than those which we witness today. The world today is filled with oppression, cruelty, hurtful problems, earthquakes, wars, starvation, and injustice—all of which begins in the pains of childbirth. Day by day the situation of our world will get worse until it reaches the end of its work.

If you tolerate persecution and come out remaining faithful, according to God's will, you will become a vessel that God can use in order to help others until they progress down this road. You can then have the courage to proclaim that you went down that road, faced those hardships, waited on the Lord, and saw Him come to your aid.

The point that I definitely want to add is found in Matthew 10:23 in which Christ says: "But when they persecute you in this city, flee ye into another;..." It is likely that some dear believers may ask why Jesus Christ gave such a command and what He meant by it. In the Bible there are other verses like this that seemingly contradict each other. There are places where a command was given to perform a specific task, and there are other places where they were commanded to stop that task. In all of these cases, just as this sentence speaks about persecution, God's meaning and the teaching of the Bible is completely clear. For example, when Jesus Christ in Matthew 5:39 says, "But I say unto you, That ye resist not evil: but whosoever shall smite thee on thy right cheek, turn to him the other also."

The opposite point is presented in James 4:7 which says, "Submit yourselves therefore to God. Resist the devil, and he will flee from you."

In Matthew, Jesus meant for the disciples not to act like wicked people, not to quarrel with them, and to be patient and peaceful with them. The subject matter in James, however, concerns our encounters with Satan as well as the temptation that comes from him; thus, we must resist it. Matthew 10:23 says, "But when they persecute you in this city, flee ye into another..." which means that if they do not recognize the message that you have been assigned to give, and decide to reject it, don't waste your time with debates, contentions, or trying to prove anything. Instead, shake the dust off of your feet and leave that place. When you try to talk about God's love with people who are not interested in divine things, are not ready to see or hear the truth, and don't think about the accuracy or inaccuracy of the things that they've heard, you must remove yourself from that kind of situation.

This, however, must never cause disappointment or discouragement while on the path of establishing truth, righteousness, and faithfulness to the Lord. Matthew 10:16 says, "Behold, I send you forth as sheep in the midst of wolves..."

Therefore, try to always be faithful to God's Word and to be a follower of truth and righteousness. Do not allow indifference, lack of attention to the Word, or weakness in doing the Lord's work create a defect in your pure and holy life as well as a negative attitude towards Christianity. Be faithful to what is true and righteous, just as Jesus Christ, who is the way, the truth, and the life. There is no other way to the presence of God other than through Jesus Christ. Do not fear persecution but rather wait on the Lord who said that He will never forsake you.

The Lack of Persecution

The lack of persecution means that in today's society, there exists false teaching regarding health and wealth.[1] This charming slogan means

---

1 The Prosperity Theology (also known as the Prosperity Gospel, the Health and Wealth Gospel, or the Success Gospel), is a religious belief that exists among some Christians. They believe that it is always God's will for them to receive financial blessings and good physical health. They also believe that positive thinking and the giving of alms will result in an increase in wealth. The Prosperity Theology sees the Bible as a type of contract between God and mankind which conveys that if mankind has faith in God, God will grant them safety and success. This belief, regarding power and success, emphasizes that God's will for His nation is joy. Sickness and poverty result from a lack of faith. During the religious healing movements of the 1950s the Prosperity Gospel first came about and the religious commentators of that time referred to the Prosperity Gospel as a movement of new thinking in the 19th Century. These teachings were later revealed in the Charismatic movement, and during the 1980s found its way into televised evangelism. In the 1990s and 200s, some leaders of the Pentecostal and Charismatic movements used the Prosperity Gospel in America, and it was then spread throughout the world. Later on the Prosperity Gospel was criticized by different Christian leaders, even among Pentecostals and Charismatics. They discredited the Prosperity Gospel, acknowledging it as idol worship and a violation of the Bible.

that if you come to church and put your faith in Jesus Christ, you will never get sick, or become poor.

It is for this reason that when the false teachers who spread this doctrine get sick, they go to the hospital at night so that no one notices. Jesus Christ clearly proclaimed that there will be hardships for you in this world. In John 15:20 Jesus says, "Remember the word that I said unto you, The servant is not greater than his lord. If they have persecuted me, they will also persecute you; if they have kept my saying, they will keep yours also." How can we say that no persecution should exist in the lives of Christians? This kind of teaching is useful for those who only want the blessings of Jesus as opposed to Jesus Himself. Let us not forget that blessings are inseparable from the lives of believers; however, we must see whether our explanation of blessings agrees with the Bible or not.

There is no arguing that peace and joy are fruits of the Spirit of God; however, just as it was pointed out previously, the joy of the Bible and the happiness of the world are completely different. Health and healing can be obtained through prayer if it is God's will; however, does this mean that sickness, or God's lack of answering our prayers for healing mean that we are cursed? Absolutely not. The Apostle Paul who by the power of the name of Jesus Christ performed many miracles, asked God three times to heal his body (a type of bodily injury from Satan) and instead of healing God responded by saying "my grace is sufficient for thee." Ask no further.

This teaching that a devout Christian will never undergo persecution, but rather that a flood of spiritual, bodily, and financial blessings will come for him, is entirely wrong. It is good to have financial conveniences; however, to be in love with money and to make it your goal in life is a complete mistake! God's Word tells us in James 4:4 that, "...know ye not that the friendship of the world is enmity with God? whosoever therefore will be a friend of the world is the enemy of God." Are we Christ's friends or enemies? The book of 1 Peter speaks entirely about the persecution and hardships of the true church of Christ as well as the role of faith in Christianity.

Another point regarding the false teachings in Christianity is the belief in the Prosperity Gospel. 1 Peter 4:19 says, "Wherefore let them that suffer according to the will of God commit the keeping of their souls to him in well doing, as unto a faithful Creator." Sometimes these hardships become real for us in the will of God. Therefore, a life in Jesus Christ will not always go the way we want it to. Sometimes when believers who live with perfect health, money, and possessions, the Lord allows persecution to come because it is in this way that we become strong and prepared. It is in these circumstances that our spiritual character takes form. The more we become like Jesus Christ, the stronger our faith becomes. In the end, we will reach a point where instead of worrying in the face of persecution, we worship the Lord with joy.

God is more interested in the development of our spiritual character as opposed to our having a comfortable life in this world. Therefore, if God's desire is for us to be more like Christ every day, then striving for truth and righteousness is the unchanging reality of our lives. Of course, while striving for truth and righteousness, it cannot be denied that we will come across hardships and troubles. It is from these hardships that the life of a believer who is seeking Christ can illustrate the Gospel, and because the people of this world hate the Gospel, they will also hate believers. You shine the light of Christ, and those who have lived their whole lives in the darkness and bondage of sin, have come to hate the light.

Imagine a person who has spent a period of time sitting in the darkness. When you open the curtains and light shines into the room, he will immediately cover his eyes and shout: "Close the curtains! Get rid of the light! My eyes hurt!" John 3:19-20 says, "And this is the condemnation, that light is come into the world, and men loved darkness rather than light, because their deeds were evil. For everyone that doeth evil hateth the light, neither cometh to the light, lest his deeds should be reproved." Therefore, if someone says that they will not witness to others in order to flee persecution, and their actions are supposed to shine like a light, what are they supposed to do? When the church is under persecution, the devout grow stronger in their faith, in their witnessing, and in living a pure and holy life because they are standing for truth and righteousness.

In contrast, believers who have more freedom and comfort usually see little to no persecution. The result is that they live a Christian life that does not meet the standards made clear in God's Word. For example, when I was serving in the ministry in Pakistan, I saw with own eyes how the Christians there lived under persecution, and how they, in the midst of these circumstances, never neglected church. They would even walk for miles in the pouring rain just to come to the services. In Los Angeles, however, people meet opportunities that they have to go to church or to witness with excuses, embarrassment, or with postponing it for another time.

The Lord sent the compassionate Jeremiah of the Old Testament to share His message, and from the very beginning reassured Jeremiah: "This nation will not listen to you words, but still speak." You might say, "Well what was the use?" Jeremiah's mission was to deliver God's message, and with faithfulness carried out this ministry. Jeremiah was beaten and tortured regularly, and thrown into a dungeon; however, he faithfully delivered God's message. Eventually a time came when he grew weary of the amount of torture and suffering and would tell himself: "Enough! I won't speak of God's message anymore and stay silent." Jeremiah 20:8-9 says, "For since I spake, I cried out, I cried violence and spoil; because the word of the Lord was made a reproach unto me, and a derision, daily. Then I said, I will not make mention of him, nor speak any more in his name..." Soon after, he regretted this thought knowing that it was impossible for him not to deliver God's message, and continued: "...But his word was in mine heart as a burning fire shut up in my bones, and I was weary with forbearing, and I could not stay" (Jeremiah 20:9). Jeremiah's facing ersecution became completely natural because he performed the task which the Lord had commanded.

Since that day nothing has changed in the world. For those who love God, all those who are faithful and true to Him, follow His Word and are seeking truth and righteousness. Not only has the situation never improved, but instead it has gotten worse. You may ask how it can be possible for things to get worse, since the world is improving every day and people now with freedom of opinion are more inclined to allow people to tolerate one another more. Today's situation compared to that of the ancient Roman Empire and their brutality is much better. We don't hear of the kind of persecution which existed during that time anymore. Today's situation, however, has gotten worse because there is more encouragement to sin. Many shameful topics and heinous acts that were only spoken of with embarrassment in private places (such as homosexuality), are now shamelessly proclaimed in the streets. It is certainly difficult for Jesus Christ, who is truth and righteousness, and for those who follow and submit to him, to tolerate this matter.

It was not only during the time of the Roman Empire that Christianity was made illegal, or that Christians were crucified upside down, or burned with branding irons. This type of persecution still continues for the disciples of Jesus Christ today.

In the last ten years, every ten minutes two people have been killed for their faith in Jesus Christ. From the time that Jesus Christ was crucified on the cross till today more than 70 million Christians have been killed solely for their faith in Jesus Christ and their faithfulness to Him. It is unbelievable that half of these people, close to 35 million people, have been killed just in the past ten years. Jesus Christ promised: "There will be hardships for you in the world. Because the world hated me it will hate you also."

Dear beloved, Satan is the master of this world. He hates God and all of His creation, especially humans, with a passion. Satan, with desire and enthusiasm, is eager to harm God, however, because it is impossible for him to do so he chooses to harm humans instead—humans that were made in the image of God, and whom God loves with a passion. The truth is that if you wish to harm a mother and father, you must try to harm their children. To strike a child is to torture his mother. In Ephesians 5:12 God's Word says, "For it is a shame even to speak of those things which are done of them in secret."

Persecution in First Peter

Let us take another look at the book of First Peter. This book specifically talks about persecution about how persecution is normal for the church. According to some Bible commentators, Peter wrote the book after the Apostle Paul's testimony in 66 AD. Silas, one of Paul's fellow laborers, then sent the book to the churches that Paul was looking after to encourage them and teach them how to tolerate the persecution that they were facing from the Roman government. Therefore, Peter's message is for the devout who are under persecution.

For the Apostle Peter, the cross is both the beginning of and the equivalent to persecution. Chapter 1 verse 18 says, "Forasmuch as ye know that ye were not redeemed with corruptible things, as silver and gold, from your vain conversation received by tradition from your fathers." The Apostle Peter then points to the cross and persecution in chapter 2 verse 24 which says, "Who his own self bare our sins in his own body on the tree, that we, being dead to sins, should live unto righteousness: by whose stripes ye were healed." Chapter 3 verse 18 also says, "For Christ also hath once suffered for sins, the just for the unjust, that he might bring us to God, being put to death in the flesh, but quickened by the Spirit:" He continues his look at persecution in chapter 4 verse 13 which says, "But rejoice, inasmuch as ye are partakers of Christ's sufferings; that, when his glory shall be revealed, ye may be glad also with exceeding joy." Therefore, the Apostle Peter's actual message to followers of Jesus, through the Spirit of God, was that we should look at persecution the same way that Jesus Christ does. The Lord uses this book to give devout believers under persecution a beautiful and rational illustration that is extremely valuable.

In 1 Peter chapter 1 verses 1-3, Peter says that those who receive salvation through the blood of Jesus Christ and faith in Him, are strangers in this world. They exist for love and goodness but instead see tribulation and persecution. The

Lord tells us in this book that the cross of Jesus is the heart of Christianity and that His afflictions are the body of Christianity. You may ask in what way. Pay attention to how God uses the death of Jesus as an example. 1 Peter 2:21 says, "For even hereunto were ye called: because Christ also suffered for us, leaving us an example, that ye should follow his steps." Also verses 22-24 say that "Who did no sin, neither was guile found in his mouth: Who, when he was reviled, reviled not again; when he suffered, he threatened not; but committed himself to him that judgeth righteously: Who his own self bare our sins in his own body on the tree, that we, being dead to sins, should live unto righteousness: by whose stripes ye were healed." Chapter 3 verse 13 tells us that "And who is he that will harm you, if ye be followers of that which is good?"

Likewise chapter 4 verses 13-14 state that "But rejoice, inasmuch as ye are partakers of Christ's sufferings; that, when his glory shall be revealed, ye may be glad also with exceeding joy. If ye be reproached for the name of Christ, happy are ye; for the spirit of glory and of God resteth upon you: on their part he is evil spoken of, but on your part he is glorified." Chapter 4 verse 19 says "Wherefore let them that suffer according to the will of God commit the keeping of their souls to him in well doing, as unto a faithful Creator."

Finally, chapter 5 verses 7-10 say, "Casting all your care upon him; for he careth for you. Be sober, be vigilant; because your adversary the devil, as a roaring lion, walketh about, seeking whom he may devour: Whom resist steadfast in the faith, knowing that the same afflictions are accomplished in your brethren that are in the world. But the God of all grace, who hath called us unto his eternal glory by Christ Jesus, after that ye have suffered a while, make you perfect, stablish, strengthen, settle you."

Therefore, those dear people who are facing persecution in Jesus Christ can be sure of the fact that their tolerating persecution as a member of the body of Christ is not in vain. Just as the persecution that Jesus tolerated was not in vain but instead bore much fruit. With Jesus' death on the cross came the remission of sins for mankind. The persecution that Jesus tolerated on the cross frees us from death and eternal condemnation and brings us from the oppression of sin into the light of God's kingdom. The persecution that Jesus faced was never in vain, because it was through his wounds that we received healing. Therefore, the persecution that you may face will not be in vain, because when you are facing persecution, the sincerity of your faith will be tested and made known. You will be rewarded for your love and faithfulness to the Lord. Your persecution is not in vain because in times of persecution, God's grace is more abundant. The hardships you face due to your faithfulness to Jesus Christ will bring you closer to Him—the Good Shepherd. 1 Peter 2:25 says "For ye were as sheep going astray; but are now returned unto the Shepherd and Bishop of your souls."

Do not forget that in times of persecution we must understand the Lord's purpose and pursue it. For example, one of God's great purposes that is exacted upon us in the midst of persecution is found in 1 Peter 3:14-15 which says "But and if ye suffer for righteousness' sake, happy are ye: and be not afraid of their terror, neither be troubled; But sanctify the Lord God in your hearts: and be ready always to give an answer to every man that asketh you a reason of the hope that is in you with meekness and fear."

Another of the Lord's purposes for persecution is found in 1 Peter 4:14 which says "If ye be reproached for the name of Christ, happy are ye; for the spirit of glory and of God resteth upon you: on their part he is evil spoken of, but on your part he is glorified." All of these verses simply tell us that for the devout, the only thing that can come from persecution is blessing.

The path of persecution for the disciples of Christ, although inevitable, will lead to blessing, glory, joy, and the ability to stand in the presence of our holy and glorious God for eternity. It is the path of the cross that is both narrow and difficult. In Matthew 16:24 Jesus says, "...If any man will come after me, let him deny himself, and take up his cross, and follow me." It is a path on which you will always be unjustly condemned and persecuted. This subject is pointed out in 1 Peter 2:19-21 which says, "For this is thankworthy, if a man for conscience toward God endure grief, suffering wrongfully. For what glory is it, if, when ye be buffeted for your faults, ye shall take it patiently? But if, when ye do well, and suffer for it, ye take it patiently, this is acceptable with God. For even hereunto were ye called: because Christ also suffered for us, leaving us an example, that ye should follow his steps."

How Should We React to Persecution and Those Who Persecute?

Allow me to respond as briefly as possible, and then elaborate further:

-Prayer and the grace of God
-The power of the Holy Spirit
-Understanding God's plan

I will now explain the steps that we must take when dealing with our persecutors.

Step 1: Expect persecution to come instead of being surprised by it. When you are living in a world full of wickedness, and want to be honest and just, how can you not expect the world to hate you?

Step 2: Don't be afraid of persecution, because He that is within you, the Holy Spirit, is greater than he that is in the world. Learn that the more you understand God's love, the less afraid you will be. Remember that the most damage that a persecutor can do to you is to kill your body—that which encloses your spirit. No one is able to hurt your true self which exists behind the windows of your eyes. It is for this reason that God's Word in Luke 12:4-5 says, "...Be not afraid of them that kill the body, and after that have no more that they can do. But I will forewarn you whom ye shall fear: Fear him, which after he hath killed hath power to cast into hell; yea, I say unto you, Fear him."

Learn to submit yourself to God more, to know Him more, and to trust Him more until you are able to worship Him in the face of persecution. Just as it is said in 1 Peter 3:14-15, "But and if ye suffer for righteousness' sake, happy are ye: and be not afraid of their terror, neither be troubled; But sanctify the Lord God in your hearts: and be ready always to give an answer to every man that asketh you a reason of the hope that is in you with meekness and fear."

Step 3: Don't be ashamed. You should never be ashamed of being faithful to the truth or of standing for righteousness. Do not allow anyone to mock you for living the right way. This does not mean that you should enter into confrontation. Instead it means that you should not allow their ridicule to make you feel ashamed. You should be proud of yourself. 1 Peter 4:16 says, "Yet if any man suffer as a hristian, let him not be ashamed; but let him glorify God on this behalf." Chapter 5 verse 9 says, "...the same afflictions are accomplished in your brethren that are in the world." 1 Peter 3:16-17 says, "Having a good conscience; that, whereas they speak evil of you, as of evildoers, they may be ashamed that falsely accuse your good conversation in Christ. For it is better, if the will of God be so, that ye suffer for well doing, than for evil doing." You can not act in such a way that will please everyone in the world. You must choose between pleasing God and pleasing men. Just as Jesus says in Mark 8:38, "Whosoever therefore shall be ashamed of me and of my words in this adulterous and sinful generation; of him also shall the Son of man be ashamed, when he cometh in the glory of his Father with the holy angels."

Step 4: Know the source of persecution. Revelation 12:10 says, "...the accuser of our brethren is cast down, which accused them before our God day and night." Therefore, men are not your enemies. Your true enemy is Satan—he who hates God and all that belongs to Him and who tries to destroy Him. Satan uses those who do not have the protection of the Holy Spirit in Jesus Christ as instruments to harm other people.

You must understand this reality that Satan uses the instruments of this world that he has control over, such as music, movies, films, and media in order to harm, harass, torture, insult, belittle, and kill Christians. Have you ever paid attention to the fact that in many American Hollywood films, the extremists or the psychopath killers and murderers are Christians? Therefore, our battle, as described in Ephesians 6, is not with men—they are only instruments in the hands of Satan because God's Spirit through Jesus Christ is not in them.

Therefore, they are totally defenseless against Satan. He can use them in any way he chooses. Persecuting devout Christians is one of the ways in which Satan uses them. Satan uses his instruments to insult, belittle, and even kill believers. It is for this reason that 2 Timothy 2:23-25 tells us to help them until they see the truth.

Step 5: Do not respond to evil with evil. According to what God's Word says in 1 Peter 2:23, we should not respond to evil at all. Jesus Christ's response to those who said that He had a demon in him, that He was under the influence of Satan, and that He was drunk, as well as those who cursed him on cross, was silence. Regarding this matter, God's Word tells us in Romans 12:17-21 that the instructions for our lives have been given to us, we must overcome evil with good. This is a very difficult task. I want you to pay special attention to the idea of not responding to evil. If you respond, you give full control to your persecutor. Sometimes we say: "I didn't want to get angry, but they forced me," but in reality you are admitting that they have control over you. On the other hand, some say: "They did____so much that I now hate them for it." Thus you give your persecutor control over your actions.

Step 6: Christianity is different than all the other religions, philosophies, and mindsets. Luke 6:27-37 talks about loving your enemies and praying for them. This kind of teaching never existed in the world before Christ. The teachings of the world always involved destroying your enemies, becoming enemies with those that hate you, and seeking vengeance. If someone slaps you across the face, you respond with a fist. If someone borrows from you and can't return it, humiliate them. Anyone can withstand hardships, but not everyone has the strength to do what God's Word says in the book of Luke. If you respond to your persecutors according to God's Word, you will first and foremost please your Heavenly Father, and then be able to show your persecutors the truth. Throughout history, the greatest enemies of Jesus Christ couldn't find any fault in Him or His behavior, instead they falsely accused Him.

It was because of Jesus Christ's behavior that the persecutor and enemy of the church-- the Apostle Paul--became the greatest Apostle of Jesus Christ and missionary of the world. As disciples of Jesus Christ, our reaction to our persecutors is explained in Romans 12:20-21 which says that we should overcome evil with good and follow the example set by our Lord and Savior Jesus Christ. The people of this world tend to act like their religious leaders, and you witness their actions. You believers of Jesus Christ, however, who through His blood have become children of God, should behave like Him. You must wear your testimony wherever you go like a beautiful gown, and spread the sweet smelling aroma of the knowledge of Christ. Do not allow your weakness and slothfulness in being holy, remaining pure, standing for truth and righteousness, and being faithful to God's Word allow enemies to find fault in Christ through you. Jesus says, "I am the way, the truth, and the life: no man cometh unto the Father but by me" (John 14:6). Do not fear persecution, but instead be faithful and fervent while waiting patiently for God to work. He is the same God that said: "I will never leave thee, nor forsake thee" (Hebrews 13:5). May the grace of Jesus Christ our Lord be with you and all believers all over the world now and forever, amen.

Pastor Firouz
November 2017

98071842R00046

Made in the USA
Columbia, SC
18 June 2018

Our mission at Calvary Chapel, and specifically at Discipleship for Iran, is to send the Gospel to the over 300 million Farsi-speaking Muslims that reside in different parts of the world.

In addition to sending God's Word, we work to train and equip Iranian house church leaders by providing week-long seminars for them outside Iran (in places such as Turkey, Armenia, and Tajikistan) When these leaders return to Iran, they can then carry out fruitful ministries within the local house churches.

Please join us in praying for this ministry!

If The Lord has laid it on your heart to support Discipleship for Iran, please visit our website at
www.discipleshipforiran.com